10
Minute Guide to
Choosing a College

by Josep

a
alpha
books

A R C O

A Division of Macmillan Publishing
A Simon & Schuster Macmillan Company
1633 Broadway, New York, NY 10019

International Standard Book Number: 0-02-860615-9

Library of Congress Catalog Card Number: 95-080515

97 96 10 9 8 7 6 5 4 3 2 1

Interpretation of the printing code: the rightmost number of the first series of numbers is the year of the book's printing; the rightmost number of the second series of numbers is the number of the book's printing. For example, a printing code of 96-1 shows that the first printing of the book occurred in 1996.

Printed in the United States of America

Publisher: Theresa Murtha

Managing Editor: Lisa Wolff

Series Editor: Bart Astor

Development Editor: Jennifer Perillo

Cover Designer: Lori Singer

Designer: Barbara Kordesh

Production Manager: Scott Cook

Production Team Supervisor: Laurie Casey

Indexer: Charlotte Clapp

Production Team: Heather Butler, Angela Calvert, Dan Caparo, Kim Cofer, David Garratt, Aleata Howard, Erika Millen, Scott Tullis, Christine Tyner, Karen Walsh

CONTENTS

INTRODUCTION

Let's get started making one of the major decisions you'll face in your life. Obviously, choosing a college takes an investment of considerably more time than these 10-minute lessons. But this guide will get you going. It will help you use the time you have to your best advantage—whether you are beginning early in your high school years or have waited until your senior year.

WHY THE 10 MINUTE GUIDE TO CHOOSING A COLLEGE?

The *10 Minute Guide to Choosing a College* suggests a process, a series of steps for you to take that will lead to choosing the right college. Each lesson will introduce important topics, and it will take you 10 minutes or so to grasp the basics of each lesson. By the time you are done with all the topics, you'll have mastered the important concepts for a thorough and successful college search. While you may be tempted to jump around and explore different questions, you should start at the beginning and work your way through, since there is a sequential logic to the suggested steps.

CONVENTIONS USED IN THIS BOOK

The *10 Minute Guide to Choosing a College* uses the following icons to identify helpful information.

Useful Tip icons offer ideas that cut corners and avoid confusion.

Plain English icons appear to define new terms.

Panic Button icons identify potential problem areas and how to solve them.

Five Encouraging Points as You Start

- There is no "perfect college" that is right for every student reading this book.

- For each one of you, there are dozens of schools that will match your interests and serve you well.

- Of the approximately 3,000 universities and colleges in the country, most are looking for students just like you.

- Finding the right school requires a commitment of your time.

- Your time will be well rewarded.

THE AUTHOR

Joseph Allen is the Dean of Admission and Financial Aid at the University of Southern California in Los Angeles, CA. Previously he was the Dean of Admission at the University of California, Santa Cruz.

ASSESSING YOURSELF

In this lesson you will learn the first step in choosing a college and questions you can ask yourself that identify what you want from college.

DECISIONS, DECISIONS

For most of you, there are two ways decisions have been made in your life:

1. by your parents or other adults

2. by your peers

So far, most of the big decisions in your life—where you live, where you go to school, where you worship—have been made by someone else, usually your parents or some other adult. Most other decisions—how you dress, who you hang out with, the kind of music you listen to, how you spend your time— have been heavily influenced by your peer group—your friends.

CHOOSING COLLEGE AS PERSONAL LIBERATION

So at this point, if the big decisions have been either controlled by the adults in your life or made in alignment with your peers, now what?

> **!** **Decision Making and College Planning.** Neither of the two ways of decision making you've encountered so far in your life are going to work in helping you make the big college decision.

Your parents cannot possibly know on their own which colleges are right for you. As for your friends, well, do you want to extend high school for the rest of your life? Now is the time in your life when you can differentiate yourself, define your own interests, and begin a new stage in your life. It can be liberating.

> **!** **Important Questions.** For many of you, deciding which college to attend will be the first major decision you make for yourself. That means that *you* get to answer the important questions.

"WHAT DO YOU WANT FROM COLLEGE?"

Every year the American Council on Education asks this question of about one million college freshmen across the country. The variety of answers is stunning:

- to improve their minds
- to make money
- to get a better job
- to make a difference in the world
- to bring about world peace
- to end starvation
- to find a cure for AIDS

While the range of responses may seem chaotic, the strength of the American system of higher education is that it can meet the needs of many different kinds of students seeking different goals.

But now *you* get to answer the question of what you want from college, and no one but you can fully answer it.

tip **Assess Yourself.** The college selection process has to start with you, making a careful assessment of your needs, goals, strengths, and weaknesses.

Assessing your goals doesn't mean you necessarily have to know what you want to do for the rest of your life. Nor does it mean you must know exactly what you want to study. Some students do, and that may lead them to make decisions about certain colleges. But most students at age 17 or 18 have very little idea about what they want to study in college. That is a healthy state of being.

QUESTIONS TO ASK YOURSELF

Every person has a unique set of skills, values, goals, and beliefs. Spend some time thinking about your own. Here are
some questions you can ask yourself:

- Do you want training for a particular career, or are
  you more interested in exploring a variety of options?

- Are you motivated by a desire to improve conditions in the world through health, education, or
  public policy?

- Are religious values important to you in your education?

- In what subjects do you do well?

- Do you particularly enjoy working with people?

- Do you prefer dealing with analytical problems?

- Are you gregarious, and do you enjoy meeting
  people?

- Do you prefer the company of a few close friends
  to knowing many different kinds of people?

> ***tip*** **Make a List.** Begin making a list of the things that matter most to you. It can be free-form, or you can use a grid—whatever works best—but get started thinking about these issues. Talk with your trusted friends and family, teachers, and counselors as you try to sort your feelings.

ANOTHER WAY

If you are not comfortable making your own list, there are several "assessment tests" that your counselor should be able to offer, including the Jackson Interest Inventory Test or the Holland Self-Directed Search Test. These tests provide a more structured format for exploring these questions.

By whatever means, clarifying your own interests, skills, values, and goals will lead you to narrow the field of college choices. It is an important first step in the process.

SUMMARY

In this lesson you learned that the first step in choosing a college is assessing yourself. You also learned some questions you can ask yourself to identify what you want from college.

Working with Your Family

In this lesson you will learn how to develop some strategies for working with your family in choosing a college.

Discussing the College Decision

Once you've begun to sort out your own thoughts about what you want from college, and you have a fairly clear idea of what you're looking for in a college, the next thing you need to do is bring your family into the decision-making process.

Typically, parents and students go on marathon college visits sometime during the college-selection process. They spend days and days together, traveling on planes, trains, and automobiles; balancing maps, college guides, and fast food; visiting as many schools as possible in just a few days.

For many families, this trip is the longest sustained period of time they've spent together for many years. And there they sit, in a hotel room, or even in an admission office, exhausted from the ordeal and thoroughly confused about what brought them to this point. Yet, despite all those hours together, discussing colleges, SATs, grades, and admission policies, many

7

families leave out of the conversation anything about their expectations for you.

> **!** **Communication.** The time for your family to communicate their expectations or wishes for your college selection to you is not when you're in the midst of visiting colleges, but well before. Share with them what you are looking for in college and ask for their advice.

Sometimes, while the family is visiting colleges, during a conversation with an admission officer a great deal of new information emerges—information about you that your parents never knew. One father was astonished to learn that his son, whom he had assumed would be following his lead into the world of business, had a consuming interest in the history of art and dreamed of being a curator at a major museum. In another case, a young woman brought equal surprise to the face of her parents by declaring her interest in geology—they had always assumed she would major in biology and head for medical school.

Few families begin discussing these issues early enough in the selection process.

> ***tip*** **Expectations.** The best time to talk with your parents about your college selection is as early as possible, and certainly before you've narrowed your list.

Whether or not your parents went to college, they will still have opinions based on their own considerations and concerns. For example, your parents generally know how far from home they consider to be an acceptable distance. Some parents will want you close; for others, that's not a major consideration. The same can be true regarding campus housing, the safety of the area, and many other details about college life. For sure, most parents have a pretty good idea of the costs they are willing to bear.

> **!** **Honesty Is the Best Policy.** Tell your parents that the best thing they can do for you is to be honest about their dreams, their hopes for you, and their bottom lines.

Have a Ground-Rule Conversation

A key step in your college-selection process is a ground-rule conversation with your parents. Have it as early as you can in the process.

> **tip** **Make a Date.** Set a specific date, time, and place for your ground-rule meeting. Tell your parents what it's for, bring your list of what you want from college, and ask them to do the same.

Both you and your parents should be ready to put all considerations on the table.

You:

- tell them what your dreams and expectations are for college
- name specific college names, if you have them
- talk about what you need from college
- tell them what you hope to accomplish in college
- tell them why you want to be close to home or 3,000 miles away from it
- be prepared to express and explain your feelings

They:

- tell you the same things
- tell you what their cost limits are
- tell you how much they are willing to borrow
- tell you how much they expect you to contribute

None of these points are particularly easy to discuss at this point, at least for most families. But they're even more difficult to deal with later.

tip   **Harmony.** The idea is to align your expectations with those of your parents from the earliest point. From there, all the energy you put into this process will be more focused.

A WORD TO PARENTS

If you are a parent who happens to be reading this book, there's a message here: this isn't your turn. Here's an exquisite irony: We spend our lives raising our children to lead independent lives, but as soon as they begin to show true signs of independence we hold on as hard as we can.

> **!** **The College Decision.** The college decision is your child's. It's a hard separation to make, and few parents are successful at completely focusing on the needs of their children in this process. But it's important to keep trying.

Parents must also be honest about another part of this process. They likely feel certain pressures as they compare the college choices available to their son or daughter to those of others, perhaps the children of friends and other family members. Cocktail parties and picnics can be nasty affairs during the college-admission season.

> **!** **Dreams and Goals.** You may have long-held dreams of your own about a particular college or career path for your child. Don't let those feelings overwhelm the process. Focus on the special needs, abilities, and goals of your child.

AN EXERCISE FOR PARENTS

Here's one exercise that's not very easy: Think back to yourself at your child's age, as you were trying to make decisions that were best for you. What kind of support did you need?

THREE APPROPRIATE ROLES FOR PARENTS

1. Be a mirror. You have a unique perspective. No matter what sort of relationship you have with your child, you've been in a position to observe her or him at close range. If she says, "I think I'm going to Berkeley," and you're thinking, "No way. Berkeley's too big; she'll be lost in the crowd," try to keep your cool. Then, reflect back to her what you have observed over the years. It may sound something like this: "I've noticed that you usually liked the smaller classes in high school and that you often said that's the way you learn best— when you know your classmates and the instructor well. Do you think that will be true in college?" Then listen. She may say that she's given that a lot of thought, is bored with the scale of her school, and looks forward to the stimulation of a larger environment. Or, she may think about what you've said and agree to pursue a smaller school. Either way, you have been of help.

2. Be realistic. You have to be honest about your family resources. There is nothing more painful than having your child gain admission to a school only to find that the cost is prohibitive for your family.

Be realistic also in your goals for your child; you do not want to push for schools that are completely out of reach. Be clear about your bottom lines regarding which are acceptable schools and how far they can be from home.

> **!** **Help with Costs.** It's a good idea for parents to do some advance work of their own on the issues of college financing. Lesson 9 of this book is a good beginning. Another book in this series, the *10 Minute Guide to Paying for College*, is a good resource.

3. Be an encourager. This is a process where nagging doesn't work. Remember, this is a very stressful time for all of you. An important role for parents is to encourage your son or daughter, pointing out areas of strength and skill that you think will be attractive to colleges.

Summary

In this lesson you learned how to develop strategies for working with your family in choosing a college.

GETTING STARTED: YOUR ROLE

In this lesson you'll learn how to take charge of the college search and application process.

Searching for the right college plus getting a handle on the application process for admission and financial aid requires a ton of paperwork and involves numerous deadlines. You must organize yourself for the process.

> **!** **Organization by Parents.** If you don't take organizing for the college selection process seriously and develop a system for keeping it all straight, you're inviting your parents to do it all for you.

In some cases, having parents heavily involved in organizing the college selection process is a good idea; that is, as long as everyone in the family has agreed early in the process on a division of responsibilities. Parents are often in a better position to make phone calls to arrange visits, for instance. With careful planning, you can form a workable partnership with your parents to see that all the tasks are accomplished.

However, if you want to take charge of this important decision yourself, you need to establish that as a ground rule and you also need to be organized, keeping the information you receive in neat, easily accessible files.

Tips to Help You Control Your Role in the Process

Here are some tips to help you maintain an appropriate role in this important process:

- Too much stuff? Set up a simple filing system, with folders for each school you are considering. Post a list on your bathroom mirror, refrigerator, or other place you look at each day with important dates and tasks. Keep a notebook with key information that you've learned from college literature, guides, college visits, and other sources.

- Be a pioneer. In our designer-label culture, we often give the most weight to names and brands that we know best. In searching for a college, this can be a very limiting way of thinking. There are more than 3,000 universities and colleges in this country, and most of them are looking for students just like you. You will be rewarded if you look beyond the obvious choices.

- Be choosy. Evidence shows that students who have been very careful in their searches, looking for the qualities they want instead of simply "name colleges," are among the most satisfied and successful in college.

- Take charge. This is the one appropriate role that most students don't believe can be accomplished. From where you sit, it seems as though someone else, usually the admission officers at the schools you want to get into, are in charge. Part of that is true: admission officers make a final decision about your application. But the fact is that choices you have made throughout your life and decisions you make now can give you a great deal of control over the college admission decision.

> ***tip*** **You Can Influence Admission Decisions.** Admission decisions are based on the information that has resulted from the countless decisions you have made.

DECISIONS YOU MAKE THAT INFLUENCE ADMISSION

You make many decisions during high school that have a great deal of influence on whether you will be admitted to the college of your choice. Here are a few:

- how challenging the courses you opt to take through school are

- how hard you study for classes and exams

- how much you prepare for the SAT

- how much effort you put into the admission process and your application

While it would perhaps be easier to believe that your fate is in the hands of others, the truth is that you are the person in control.

SUMMARY

In this lesson, you learned why it's important for you to take charge of your college search and you learned some steps to help you do so.

4

GETTING THE INFORMATION YOU NEED FROM PEOPLE

In this lesson you'll learn how to identify key people and get in-depth information from them to help you learn about colleges you might be interested in attending.

SOME KEY PEOPLE

There are five key people from whom you can get critical information that will help you in your college selection decision-making process:

- high school guidance counselors
- private counselors
- college admission officers
- alumni
- currently enrolled students

19

YOUR HIGH SCHOOL GUIDANCE COUNSELOR

If you're fortunate enough to attend a high school that has a college guidance department, you should definitely make this your first stop. Your college counselor can save you countless hours of research time. These counselors are experts in the field and can be a great resource for you.

> ***tip*** **A Golden Relationship.** The relationship you have with your guidance counselor is important. You can make the most of this relationship if you contact your counselor early and often. Bring the product of all the work you have been doing to clarify your goals.

The counseling office also schedules visits from college representatives and can tell you about test dates, college fairs, financial aid workshops, and other events important to you. Most counselors also maintain files with publications from various colleges and have a library of college guides.

> **!** **Plan Ahead.** Remember that most counselors are overworked and have many other students to serve. Don't wait until the last minute to ask your counselor to write a letter on your behalf, send your grades, or fill out a recommendation form.

Seeking Out Private Counselors?

Many high schools, both public and private, don't have adequate college-counseling staffs. This is especially true of school districts that are experiencing severe budget crunches. In these situations, some families may turn to private counselors, who typically charge a fee for their services. As in any other business, some practitioners are quite good and others are not. It's best to ask around, get references, and be certain that the private counselor is associated with a regional or national association. It is also important to negotiate all fees in advance.

> **!** **The Private Counselor "Look."** Don't allow the private counselor to "package" you for a college. Admission officers want you to represent yourself.

If you need a private counselor, here are two nonprofit organizations that you may contact with questions about independent counselors:

> National Association of College Admissions
> Counselors
> 1800 Diagonal Road, Suite 430
> Alexandria, VA 22314
> (703) 836-2222
>
> The Independent Educational Consultants
> Association
> 4085 Chain Bridge Road, Suite 401
> Fairfax, VA 22030
> (703) 591-4850

HELP FROM THE EXPERTS: COLLEGE ADMISSION OFFICERS

Many colleges and universities send admission officers to individual high schools and college fairs in your area. Check first with the counseling office in your school to see whether a particular college's representative will be visiting your area. If your counselor doesn't know of a planned visit, call the admission office of any college in which you have interest and ask if they plan to have a representative in your area. Often, the people you speak with on the phone are the same people who will later read your application and recommend action on your admission. So, in addition to asking them for information, let them know who you are.

ALUMNI

If the school is some distance away and it's not possible for you to see an admission officer from the school, call the admission office and ask if they have a designated alumni representative in your area. Many campuses use alumni in this way, and alumni can often be helpful in providing information about the school. They may also conduct interviews that can help you get admitted.

> **!** **Out of Touch.** A caution: some alumni have been away from their alma maters for many years, and while they are still a valuable resource, they may be unable to talk about the campus as it is today.

CURRENTLY ENROLLED STUDENTS

Students currently enrolled at the college can be one of the best resources to get information about a particular campus. They can tell you about the current culture on campus, the education they're receiving, the availability of the professors, classes, activities, and so on. Most important, they can relate to what you're going through and can let you know whether the information and preconceived notions you have about the college are accurate. On the other hand, their view of reality will be clouded by their personal experiences: whether they've made friends, or how well they're doing in classes. Anecdotal information about a college can provide great insight. It is also just one person's experience that may or may not be what you can expect.

tip   **College Visits.** If you're visiting a college, be sure to talk with students while you're there (and not just the tour guides). You can expect them to be candid about the things they like and those that could be improved.

SUMMARY

In this lesson you learned about people who can help you with your college search.

Getting Information from Other Sources

In this lesson you will learn how to find information to help you in your college search.

Sources of Information Outside the Colleges

Besides people, there are other, more objective sources of information that will help you in your college selection process. You can find these sources in your library, college center/guidance office, bookstores, and cyberspace:

- published college guides
- college search computer programs
- Internet guides and college home pages
- magazines

GETTING THE MOST FROM PUBLISHED COLLEGE GUIDES

There are several well-known and respected objective guide-books that you can borrow from your counselor or library or purchase at a bookstore. They can be a great source of basic information such as:

* size of college
* number of applicants
* number of students accepted
* cost
* location
* majors available
* facilities
* housing
* average SAT or ACT score of students
* degree of difficulty of getting in

These books offer excellent information on just about every college in the country. This data can help you enormously in beginning your search. College guides can also help you narrow down your list of potential colleges. You'll definitely want to review them *with* your parents.

tip Published College Guides. Published college guides typically give you only some basic facts, not enough information to base your college decision on. Use them to help you get started, but not as your sole source.

The real questions you have to ask yourself about published college guides are, How accurate are they? and How should I use them?

Let's say you're looking up a few colleges in one of the books to find out whether you could get accepted or not. One of the criterion will be your scores on the standardized tests (SAT or ACT).

Let's suppose further that a college lists an "average" SAT score, and your scores fall within that range. And let's suppose you're interested in majoring in the sciences or math. Does the "average" SAT score the college reports reflect just science majors? Or does it also include music and drama majors for whom the only criterion that counts for admission at that college is the student's performance at an audition?

! Subjective College Guides. There are dozens of guides that interject opinions and subjective analysis of campuses. These so-called insider guides are lively and make good reading. Some are reasonably accurate, but others are way off.

Let's consider another example—one of the subjective guide-books where the descriptions of campus life may be written by current students or recent graduates. Let's say a certain college is listed as being one of the top 10 party schools. Does that really mean that at a campus of 20,000 or 30,000 students everybody is partying all night? On the other hand, is a school whose description contains absolutely no mention of its social life just for nerds? Let's be realistic. Can you really sum up a college in just a few words? Weigh subjective descriptions in college guides carefully.

tip   **Special Interests?** There are also college guides that will help you assess the right college for specialized interests, such as the *K and W Guide to Colleges for the Learning Disabled.* If you have concerns about such things as minority student life, women's issues, athletics, or outdoor activities, you will find college guides that will help you.

COMPUTER SEARCHES

Every day more and more college search computer programs appear on the market. For the most part, these are college guides on disk—some with photos, video, or sound, and some without.

But, because they're interactive databases, these programs offer the ability to sort through thousands of colleges quickly and in a logical way. They can lead you through your selection of possible colleges by location, cost, distance from home, size, academic and extracurricular programs, and how hard it is to get in (often called "degree of competitiveness"). If, for example, you want to know what medium-size colleges in a particular region of the country offer a biomedical engineering major, you won't have to read through a printed directory to find a match. The computer will do the sorting for you.

Some of the newer versions are on CD-ROM and contain bits of video and audio about the colleges. These products look and sound pretty slick but are quite limited. Each video takes up some 30 to 50 megabytes of memory, so even multiple CDs can't show more than a snippet about each college.

> **!** **Search Programs Contain Limited Information.** By their nature, computerized college search programs can't give you a full description of a college. They're essentially college guides on disk, and they have the same limitations.

Again, like collegxe guides, these programs are a good place to start your college search but should by no means be the only source of information you use.

There are several different computerized college search programs available in bookstores and, probably, in your high school guidance office or public library.

SEARCHING IN CYBERSPACE

Several college guides are now accessible on the Internet, and others will be coming online soon. If you have access to the

Internet, surf a bit, and you may find some interesting information.

Most colleges have already put up their own "home pages" on the World Wide Web (or will be doing so soon) portion of the Internet. These home pages provide everything from the course catalog to photos of their campuses.

tip **No Connection?** If you can't get into cyberspace at home or school, try your local library. This is an exciting way to get information.

MAGAZINE RANKINGS

We live in a society where nearly every commercial product, city, or service is evaluated and then ranked in some sort of best-to-worst order. Lately, magazines like *U.S. News and World Report* and *Money* have been ranking colleges and universities. You should be careful in using such rankings for the following reasons:

- Colleges and universities are complex institutions. They do not lend themselves to simple analysis.

- The information the magazines use comes from the colleges themselves.

So, of what use are rankings? Like most other surveys, they can give you some sense of direction. However, they cannot give you the full information you need to make careful decisions.

> **!** **Using School Rankings.** Suppose there was some agreement on a way of identifying the best college in America. Would that make it the right college for you? The best college for you is the one that meets *your* personal criteria.

MATERIALS FROM THE COLLEGES

Most universities and colleges are actively recruiting students, and many will send materials directly to you—incredible amounts of stuff. If you've taken the PSAT and have indicated that you would like to receive information from colleges interested in you, get ready. Your mailbox will be flooded from the spring of your junior year through the fall.

The first mailing is typically called a "search piece," and its purpose is to give you some basic information, hoping you will respond with a mail-back card. If you do, you will be placed on that school's mailing list and you'll receive a view book, catalog, application, and financial aid materials. You may also receive a video about the campus.

> **!** **College Brochures.** All the brochures and materials colleges send you are, of course, self-promotional. They should be taken with a grain of salt. But pay attention to application and financial aid information, especially about application deadlines for admission, financial aid, and scholarships.

COLLEGE FAIRS

Most high schools sponsor college fairs (or college nights), to which many colleges send representatives to staff a booth for a couple of hours, hand out literature, and talk with potential students. Sometimes, a few high schools will organize a fair together, particularly if the schools are relatively small and close together.

In addition, the National Association of College Admissions Counselors (NACAC) sponsors events held throughout the country, to which 50 to 100 colleges send representatives to speak with students and parents. And, sometimes, your state association of college admission counselors will organize a college fair.

These are excellent places to gather information, both in written form and by word of mouth.

tip   **Alumni Reps.** There are thousands of college fairs held throughout the country during the fall and the spring. Colleges can't send admission representatives to all of them, so they rely on local alumni. Look back a couple of pages and read what we said about getting information from alumni.

SUMMARY

In this lesson you learned how to gather information about colleges that will help you in your college selection decision.

6

CHOOSING AN OPTION

In this lesson you will get an overview of the types of opportunities you have after you complete high school.

TYPES OF SCHOOLS

Most books that deal with college admission, like this one, use the term "college" to cover most post–high school options. In fact, however, the term "college" has a specific meaning, and you may not even want to attend a college but would prefer some other form of post-secondary education.

Here are some options to consider with respect to your post–high school education and some important information about each:

- colleges or universities
- public or private
- religious or no affiliation
- men's and women's colleges
- historically black colleges
- specialized schools

- technical and/or vocational schools
- military academies

A COLLEGE OR UNIVERSITY: WHAT'S THE DIFFERENCE?

Generally, *colleges* are smaller schools that emphasize the liberal arts and focus primarily on undergraduates. Most do not specialize in career or vocational training but in providing a strong base of education across the disciplines. Almost all have general education requirements and ensure that all students have exposure to the natural sciences, social sciences, arts, and humanities. The basic notion of a liberal arts education is that it prepares students to think critically, communicate well, and solve problems from a variety of perspectives.

A *university* typically has a "college of liberal arts" or "college of letters, arts, and sciences" in addition to a number of professional colleges specializing in subjects such as engineering, medicine, and business. Depending on size and mission, they may have many more professional and graduate programs in a variety of fields. And, usually, there is a much broader range of majors and minors from which to choose.

There are no simple answers as to which situation is best for an individual student, but some general rules apply.

Choose a college if:

- you are the type of person who learns best in a more intimate setting
- you want a place where you will know your fellow students and faculty well

- you want a place where the atmosphere is more familiar

Choose a university if:

- you enjoy the stimulation and relative anonymity of a larger setting

- you want many options to choose from

- you want a place where you are likely to meet new people every day

PUBLIC VERSUS PRIVATE

Public colleges and universities are institutions supported by state or local tax dollars. As a result, the tuition and fees are usually considerably less for state residents. Private schools may also receive some public funds (federal and state student financial aid, research grants, etc.) as well as private donations, but compared to public universities they are more like private businesses: their "customers" have to pay the expenses of running the show.

Many people assume that private education offers superior opportunities to the public sector. This is emphatically not true! It would be ridiculous to say that private colleges and universities are "better" than those that are publicly supported. Just think about the many public campuses that have achieved greatness—the University of California at Berkeley, the University of Michigan, and the University of Texas, to name just three.

Limited funds for public colleges, however, mean that financially healthy private colleges may give you better access to classes and majors. This means that you're better able to graduate within the traditional four years. If you are selecting a public college, it is important to know the status of state and government support for that institution.

RELIGIOUS AFFILIATIONS

There are many colleges and universities that are affiliated with a particular church or religious group. Some maintain very strong affiliations and reflect the values of their sponsors. Some require a chapel service or particular courses for all students, while others may have strong rules about social behavior. If you are interested in a specific type of religious affiliation, start with your local clergy. They are often in a good position to advise you about opportunities.

> **tip**
>
> **Strength of Affiliation.** Don't automatically write off a school because its religious affiliation is different from yours. Ask admission officers how many students are not members of the religious group.

MEN'S AND WOMEN'S COLLEGES

These colleges are devoted to focusing on their students' personal, social, and academic development. Some students may find the atmosphere at these colleges more conducive to developing leadership skills and "bonding" with fellow students.

Historically Black Colleges

In addition to strengthening the personal, social, and academic development of students, these colleges offer a broad exposure to black culture. They also offer students many networking opportunities.

Specialized Schools

These schools are different from colleges in the way they approach learning. They allow you to pursue your interests with single-minded devotion, usually in the arts, music, business, or engineering. Students attending these schools have a strong and nearly exclusive interest in their field and intend to pursue this interest professionally after they complete their education. They are not attending school to get a comprehensive education.

There are many fine specialized schools. If you are interested in applying to any, your teachers in your field of interest can often help you learn about which ones are for you.

> **!**
>
> **Choosing a Specialized School.** When choosing to attend a specialized school, be certain of your interest. You will be prepared with depth rather than breadth, and if your interests change or broaden, it may be necessary to transfer to another type of school.

TECHNICAL AND VOCATIONAL SCHOOLS

Another option that many students consider after high school (or even much later in life) is attending a school that offers training for a specific job. If your interests are related to a specific skill or career ambition, there are many fine technical and vocational schools that will concentrate on preparing you for the world of work. Vocational schools that specialize in aeronautics, fashion design, photography, culinary studies, mechanics, and many other fields boast very high placement rates for their graduates into career opportunities.

!
Caution. When choosing a vocational or technical school to attend, be very cautious. While there are many excellent legitimate schools, there are an equal number of rip-offs. Your guidance counselor or school librarian has resources that can help you select a good program.

MILITARY ACADEMIES

These schools emphasize military and technical fields as well as physical fitness and training. Students and their families do not have to pay for education at the federal military academies (tuition and fees are paid by the government), but students do agree to serve in the military for a certain number of years after graduation.

Summary

In this lesson you learned about the different types of opportunities you have to continue your education after high school.

THINKING ABOUT YOUR ACADEMICS

In this lesson you will learn about academic issues to consider in choosing a college.

THE OVERALL LEARNING ENVIRONMENT

Choosing a college is a narrowing process that starts with identifying your objectives and matching them with institutions that can help you meet those objectives. One of the key factors you want to consider in this process is how closely a college fits the learning environment you are looking for.

Some questions to ask yourself when you are evaluating a college's educational environment include:

- How demanding is the educational environment? Too demanding for you? Not demanding enough?

- Who teaches what courses? Professors? Instructors? Graduate teaching assistants?

- Does the college offer the specific major or program you are interested in?

- What is the academic advising system like? Will you have a faculty advisor assigned to you for your major?

- What are the basic or core requirements for a degree? (What courses do all students have to take?)

- What is the course selection like? Which courses are open to freshmen? What is the sequence in which courses have to be taken?

- What is the grading system?

- What are the average class sizes for introductory courses? Advanced courses?

- How good are the library facilities? Computing facilities? Other facilities related to your academic interests (e.g., laboratories for science majors)?

THE COLLEGE FACULTY

One of the most important academic issues in your college choice is who will be teaching you.

The faculty is the heart of any college or university. Ideally, in addition to doing their own scholarly work, faculty members teach undergraduates and are available to students for advising and support.

You can learn a great deal about the values of an institution by knowing who teaches. Ask an admission representative these three questions:

1. Do full professors teach in the undergraduate program?

2. What role do teaching assistants have?

3. Who teaches the general education and introductory courses most students must take?

Here's an exercise you can do that will get at the heart of who's teaching:

1. Inspect the course catalog and the schedule of classes from any school you are serious about exploring. The catalog will describe all the courses for various academic programs and list faculty members in each department.

2. Look for senior faculty members (those who are listed as full or associate professors) and their research interests—those members of the faculty you imagine would be great in a class.

3. Then, check the schedule of classes for the current semester to see who's teaching them. (Remember that not all classes are taught each semester and that research universities do have some faculty members with primary responsibilities in graduate courses and research.)

With these caveats in mind, you should be able to determine if this is a campus where undergraduate education is a priority of the faculty.

ACADEMIC PROGRAMS

IF YOU ARE LOOKING FOR A SPECIFIC PROGRAM

If you have chosen a college major or a specific career path, you already know that you have to narrow your college choice to institutions offering the appropriate programs. The college guides or search software you learned about in Lesson 5 can help you identify colleges that offer the programs you need.

You then need to determine which programs best match your expectations and needs. Below are some questions to ask to help you do this. You can find the answers in college guides or the material colleges send to you, or you can pose the questions to representatives from the colleges in which you are interested.

Ask these questions regarding specific academic programs:

- What courses are offered with the program and at what level?

- Who teaches classes at each level?

- What is the style in which classes are taught? Lectures? Small classes? Laboratories? Independent study?

- What other facilities are available to support the program?

- How large and diverse is the program faculty? What are the backgrounds of the faculty?

- How many students are in the program?

- If the program is career oriented, what have the placement rates been for graduates of the program? Are there internship programs available?

- If the program is a precursor to graduate school (such as prelaw or premed), what is the graduate school acceptance rate?

These questions should help you understand the pluses and minuses of each potential academic experience. You can then weigh them along with your overall assessment of the colleges you are considering.

IF YOU HAVEN'T DECIDED ON A MAJOR

Don't be concerned if you haven't decided on a major yet. College is a time to learn about yourself and to focus your interests toward a future profession or advanced academic pursuit. Many successful graduate students and professionals didn't select a major until after completing two years of college.

That said, you will need to focus your attention on colleges or universities that offer programs of general interest to you. That is, if you have a strong interest in mathematics and sciences, you probably won't want to choose a school with a primary focus on dramatic arts, theater, and the humanities.

You should still be asking many of the questions listed above to determine if the college or university you are considering has strong programs in the areas that interest you.

CLASS SIZE

Generations of college-seeking students have been taught to ask the question, "What is your student-to-faculty ratio?" If class size is a major concern to you in your college selection, you need to investigate beyond the usual statistics that colleges provide.

> **!** **Myth about Student-to-Faculty Ratio.** The student-to-faculty ratio does not necessarily tell you anything about class size; it reflects only the number of faculty members on staff.

If you see in the catalog that the student-to-faculty ratio is 15:1, does that mean the average class size is 15? No, it doesn't—and here's why. Every campus has a greater or lesser number of faculty members who do little or no teaching: professors on sabbatical, administrators who teach infrequently, researchers, and even the semiretired. But most colleges count these faculty members in the student-to-faculty ratio.

> **tip** **Ask about Class Size.** If you want to know the class size, why not ask what you want to know: "I'm thinking about studying biology. What is the average size of classes I'll take my first two years? The second two years?"

DOES SIZE MATTER?

Both small and large colleges offer students potentially enriching educational experiences. Each type of institution provides a wide range of benefits that only you can choose among, based on your own personality, learning style, and comfort level in different settings.

Some of the benefits small colleges offer include:

* smaller classes with more interaction with faculty members

* emphasis on personal development

* greater opportunity to participate in extracurricular activities

* a sense of community

Some of the benefits larger colleges offer include:

* great range and variety of courses

* generally more advanced facilities and resources

* more activities from which to choose

* more events on campus, such as visits from celebrity lecturers and other popular figures

Size may not be a factor for you. Some students find large classes and lecture halls the most stimulating way to learn. For these students, getting to know faculty members on a personal basis is not as important as being challenged by the material and the way it's presented. In other words, if a Nobel laureate is teaching the class, who cares how large it is?

Most high school classes are relatively small, so you may not know what a large class or a large campus would be like for you. A great way to check your reaction to class size is simply to visit a variety of campuses and sit in on classes. Talk with your friends at different colleges and ask them about their experiences. In the end, this is an issue only you can decide.

CLASS AVAILABILITY

Many students and parents ask about the availability of classes needed to complete a degree within four years. This question addresses not only academic and career goals, but also the added costs involved in an additional year or two of college.

There are many reasons why students don't graduate in four years: They take advantage of foreign study programs; they complete internships that may not carry units of credit but provide invaluable experience; or they change their majors.

If your concern is about whether you can graduate in four years, ask this: "I am going to study history. Can I get all the classes I need to graduate in four years?" This, of course, presumes you are willing to stay "on track" for four years, taking the right sequence of courses and not changing majors.

Sequence of Courses. This is the order in which courses in a program must be taken. For example, Marketing 101 must be taken before Marketing 102.

THE LIBRARY

One of the most important academic resources for students is the library, the place where you will often study and do research. Prospective students often ask, "How many volumes do you have in your library?" But if this question ever had any real meaning, it's gone now.

> **tip**
>
> **Electronic Libraries.** The relevant question for the electronic age is, "What access does your library offer to research sites and libraries across the world?"

The Internet, the World Wide Web and emerging new technologies have changed the means of access to research materials for students. You will want to know:

- Does the college offer ready access to the Internet and the World Wide Web?

- Does the college offer access to commercial on-line services such as America Online or CompuServe?

- If so, is this access in the library?

- Will my dorm room or study hall be "wired"?

The traditional library has not gone away, and it remains an important consideration. Periodical collections, printed reference works, and the availability of study halls are all vital to your success as a student.

GUIDANCE SERVICES

The most frequent student complaint on most college campuses, aside from the food, concerns who does academic advising. Nationally, about half the students who enter college in a given year are undecided about their course of study. They are "undeclared."

There's nothing wrong with being unsure of your goals while you are in the early stages of your academic career. But being undeclared places even greater emphasis on the need for strong academic advising. Students who are deciding about majors not only need help in setting their academic path; they also need advice about course requirements and prerequisites.

So find out who does academic advising:

- full-time faculty members?
- graduate students?
- professional advisors?

And be sure to ask when you will have access to academic advising.

> **tip**
>
> **Starting Here, Starting Now.** Ideally, access to academic advisors should begin before you enroll for your first set of classes and should be available to you throughout your four (or more) years.

SUMMARY

In this lesson you learned how the educational environment impacts your college choice.

GOING BEYOND ACADEMICS

In this lesson you will learn about the nonacademic factors you should consider when choosing a college.

QUESTIONS TO THINK ABOUT

You're going to be spending four, five, or more years at a school. That's a pretty long time. There are a lot of things that are important to you that have nothing to do with how good the school is academically and should, in fact, have as much influence on your decision as academics. Here are the nonacademic factors to consider when thinking about which colleges will be best for you:

- location
- student body
- security
- housing
- food

- health care
- values of the school

LOCATION

Location is an important element that students and families spend a great deal of time thinking about. In fact, more than any other single factor, location determines college choice. Why? Convenience, familiarity, and the cost of getting there are very important to many students and their families in selecting a college.

> ***tip*** **Truth and Location.** Here's the astounding truth: 85 percent of college and university students attend campus within 50 miles of home.

Part of considering location is looking for a place where you will want to live for four years. Remember, this is not a vacation site you're visiting for a week or two. If you visit Maine or Minnesota in the spring, remember that they have long winters when you have to dress in several layers of clothing to walk across the street. If you're from the Northeast or the Midwest and are thinking about attending a college in California, consider the possibility that you may find going to the beach on Thanksgiving an equally jarring experience.

Many students who come from rural areas are anxious to experience urban and suburban life. And, of course, the reverse is often true, with students from urban locations seeking campuses in bucolic settings away from cities. It's a case of the "grass always looking greener"—an understandable impulse, but is it a good strategy?

Many students who aspire to careers in certain professions find that proximity to work-study, internship, and fieldwork assignments is an important part of their education. For example, a student interested in business may hope to gain some practical experience while in college, or an aspiring actor may hope to have access to theatrical opportunities. For them, living in or near a large city is important. On the other hand, some students at rural and small-town schools find the very sense of distance from urban life refreshing and better suited to their studies and interests.

> **!** **Viewbooks and Location.** You will never see a college viewbook that fails to put the best spin on its location. Don't get too excited about a campus until you have visited it. And make sure your visit goes beyond the campus itself.

A key question to ask yourself is: How far away do you want to be from home? For students with wonderful family relationships, the thought of "moving away" can be painful. There may be grandparents or younger brothers and sisters to consider. This a very personal decision. It is useful to remember that, while air travel can seem to shorten the distance, it can be prohibitively expensive for many families.

> **tip** **Reach Out and Touch Someone.** Technology, including fax machines and electronic mail, provides quick, efficient, and inexpensive ways for students to communicate with loved ones.

On the other hand, it can be difficult to develop fully on your own if your family relationships remain the focus of your free time. Students who go home every weekend often find it difficult to engage fully in the life of the campus.

> **!** **Free at Last.** For some students, the need to get away from home can be the major motivation for attending college. Use caution here. That initial "rush" of freedom can turn to loneliness pretty quickly when you're 3,000 miles from home during the holidays.

In the end, it isn't a matter of geographic difference so much as one of attitude. There are students who go to schools within an hour's drive of home who manage to live very independent lives. Others who go to school on the opposite coast from home maintain very strong ties to their families. It's up to you and the way you plan your communication with the home front.

In sum, you need to ask yourself:

- How close to home do you need to be? Within an hour's drive? Or would getting there in three to four hours by car or train be OK?

- Can you or your family afford the cost of frequent air travel?

- If being far from home is not an issue, or if you want to be a long way from home, what climate do you prefer? What activities or sports? Do you want to be close to a major city or nowhere near one? Do you prefer being near the beach or the mountains?

THE STUDENT BODY

A key to your personal satisfaction in college will be your peers. These are the people with whom you will form lifelong friendships.

> *tip* **Student Profiles.** Almost every college admission office can give you a profile of the current freshman class. This profile should tell you about your potential classmates' academic abilities, geographic and ethnic mix, how many attended public or private high schools, and so on.

When you find out more about the other students who are attending the college, you can make a more accurate assessment of what the college is really like.

> **tip** **You and the Profile.** Does the freshman class profile describe the kind of people with whom you want to spend the next four years of your life? It's a fair question to ask.

SECURITY

Feeling safe on your college campus is a primary concern for many students and parents. And rightly so. There's been much media attention focused on crime on college campuses.

> **Campus Security Act.** In response to concerns about campus safety, the U.S. Congress passed the Campus Security Act of 1990, requiring all schools to provide comprehensive annual reports on crime statistics. These are available from every admission office or security department. This is one way to get reliable, comparable data about campus safety.

In your college search, ask these questions about services available to students:

- Is there an escort service?

- Does it operate around the clock?

- How many security officers are on duty throughout the day?

- Does the college offer personal-safety classes?
- How is access to the dorms controlled?
- Are emergency phones located throughout the campus?

Housing

Where you live is important to your academic and social life while in college. Students who live on campus often have more successful academic and social lives. They are more likely to get to know faculty members, attend campus events, and engage in the life of the college. So, you'll want to know if the campuses you're considering have adequate housing.

Campus housing facilities vary greatly from campus to campus, and there are several important factors to take into consideration during your search. Some colleges require that all first-year students live on campus (except for students who live within commuting range), while some take a more flexible approach.

The process of applying for housing also varies enormously from school to school. Some colleges, including most of the smaller liberal arts colleges, guarantee housing for all students. Larger universities, particularly public campuses, may not have enough housing for all students, and the competition for on-campus housing can be fierce. If you think you'll want to live on campus for all four years, you'll want to know if the colleges you're considering can guarantee housing for you.

! Applying for Housing. It's important to know the process of applying for housing at each college. Some require a separate application to the housing office with a small fee. Others include the housing application with your admission application. Some deal with housing before you've been accepted, some after.

Be certain that you know what housing options are available for freshmen. If you have particular interests—a French-language floor, an ethnic-theme dorm, or a quiet hall—see if you can get assigned accordingly for your first year. (Sometimes the competition for these options means that only seniors or juniors can make use of them.)

tip **Special Housing Needs.** If you have certain requirements that affect the kind of housing you'll need, make sure these needs can be accommodated in your housing request or assignment. And be certain to communicate these needs early in the housing application process. Such special needs include handicap accessibility, health conditions that require a single room, or a kosher kitchen.

Here is a list of questions to ask about campus housing:

- What percentage of students live on campus?
- Is living on campus required?

- If I choose to live on campus, is on-campus housing guaranteed?
- What kind of housing options are available—dorms, apartments, suites?
- What are the arrangements for coed and single-sex housing?
- Are there "theme" dorms or floors for special academic or social interests?
- Are the dorms "wired" for computer access to the library or campus administrative services?
- Are security measures adequate? Who has access to the dorms?
- Is there adequate fire safety—alarms and sprinklers?
- Who supervises residential life?

FOOD SERVICES

Every campus has its own set of options for where and what students eat. Colleges have meal plans where all your meals are purchased in advance (including all-you-can-eat salad bars), plans that provide two meals a day, plans that cover only weekdays . . . and the list goes on. You'll be able to choose the option that best suits you.

And, in all likelihood, if you speak with just about any student on campus, they'll all tell you the same thing: the food is terrible. (Well, after all, it's not home cooking!)

To help you get a handle on the food situation, here are questions you should ask about the food service at the college:

- What meal plans are available?
- Can I have meals across campus, or just near my residence?
- Are there unlimited servings?
- What hours are dining facilities available?
- What other facilities (coffeehouses, delis, etc.) does the campus have?

HEALTH SERVICES

Most campuses have health centers that provide emergency care and basic health services for students. The best also conduct educational programs on important health concerns such as safe sex, AIDS awareness, eating disorders, stress reduction, healthy diets, and exercise.

You'll want to know:

- What kinds of health services are available?
- How much do health services cost?
- What medical insurance plans are accepted?
- What are the credentials of the medical and clinical staff?
- What are the hours of operation of the health center?
- Does the health center have any association with other nearby health facilities?

If you have specific concerns about any health issues you may be dealing with, be certain to call or write the health center with your questions.

The Values of the Institution

Here are two questions students often do not consider, although they can be key to making a good college choice: What are the values of the college? And how do I find out what its values are?

During your search, prepare a list of the things you value most. For example:

- undergraduate education
- religious beliefs
- political convictions
- personal freedom

Most schools include "mission statements" in their catalogs that will help you determine which schools have values that match yours. You can also talk to admission representatives, current students, alumni, and faculty.

- You can tell if a college values undergraduate education by looking at course offerings and who teaches lower-level courses.

- You can gain a sense of the religious atmosphere by noting what clubs and religious organizations are active at the college.

- You can learn about the political climate by looking at the clubs and also by reading the campus

newspaper, checking out bulletin boards (to see
what's being organized), and finding out who the
guest speakers are.

- You can determine how much the institution values personal freedom by looking at the rules of
  conduct it insists students abide by.

SUMMARY

In this lesson you learned about the basic nonacademic areas
you'll want to investigate when choosing a college.

MAKING COLLEGE AFFORDABLE

In this lesson you will learn what questions you should ask about financial aid.

> **!** **The Reality of Cost.** Danger: Many students will choose colleges based on perceptions about cost and financing, not the realities. Because money is one of the subjects that families have the most difficulty talking about in an open way, it is often the biggest stumbling block to making good decisions.

COLLEGE COSTS

The cost of a college education has been rising, and that fact gets a great deal of attention in the press. Unfortunately, much less information is available in the press about financial aid and support that institutions will offer to help families meet rising costs.

Every campus offers some help to families who cannot afford the full cost of education. How they do it, and how much money they are able to offer, will vary from campus to campus.

> *tip*
>
> **Seeking Assistance.** You need to know in explicit detail the financial aid policies of each college you are considering. Each college will send you a booklet that should detail its policies, including the answers to the questions listed here.

Federally supported forms of financial aid are debated annually by the Congress and are subject to the winds of political change. Of late, this has brought about a much broader definition of need, particularly in the loan programs, as the government responded to concerns that middle-class families were struggling to pay for college. More families than ever are now eligible for support, but the key factor is the amount of money Congress appropriates for financial aid programs.

QUESTIONS YOU SHOULD ASK ABOUT COST AND FINANCIAL AID

What is the total cost of attendance for one year?

> The cost of education includes tuition, fees, room and board, books, travel, and incidental expenses. As you are comparing the cost of one institution to another, this is the figure you want.

Is the school's admissions policy "need-blind"?

> Most campuses make admission decisions without
> regard to the applicants' ability to pay. In other
> words, in considering you for admission, they are
> "blind" to family need. It is important for you to
> know if your financial situation is going to be a
> factor in the admission decision.

Does the school provide need-based and/or merit-based aid?

> These are the two basic forms of financial aid.
> *Need-based aid* is awarded according to formulas
> that weigh the total cost of attendance against
> your family's "ability to pay." Any federal govern-
> ment money will be awarded according to a com-
> mon methodology all campuses must use, but
> campuses may vary in how they award their own
> funds for need. *Merit-based aid* is awarded to stu-
> dents for significant achievement in academics or
> other talents a campus may value. If your family
> qualifies for aid on the basis of need, there is a
> standard application procedure. If your family does
> not qualify for need-based aid, then merit-based
> aid may be a way to get support. The application
> process for these funds will vary, and you need to
> ask each college about procedures.

What is the ratio of grant-to-loan in the average financial aid
package?

> Campuses provide financial aid to students in the
> form of a "package" that usually includes three

types of support: *grant,* or "gift," money, which does not have to be repaid; *loans,* which must be repaid; and *work-study funds,* which a student earns by working, usually on campus. An important variable is the amount of grant money compared to the amount of loans. It is more favorable for your package to have a higher degree of grant aid, but some amount of loan should be expected.

Does the college meet full demonstrated financial need?

After determining an individual student's "need," some campuses are able to provide a financial aid package that covers the full amount. Other campuses cannot and leave a "gap" in the package that the student must cover from other funds.

These questions will get you started as you consider cost as one element in your search for a college. For more information on the subject of financial aid, read William Van Dusen's *10 Minute Guide to Paying for College.*

SUMMARY

In this lesson you learned how you can take advantage of financial aid and five key questions you can ask about financial aid.

NARROWING
YOUR LIST

In this lesson you will learn how to narrow the list of possible schools.

CHARTING YOUR DECISION

Now comes the time when you have to make the tough decisions and eliminate some of the schools you've been considering. It's not an easy task. But one way that helps many students is using a grid. Follow these steps, using the chart provided in Appendix B as a model:

1. Going down the left side of a page, abbreviating as necessary, list all the criteria that are most important to you in a college. It may include four or five items, or even thirty. But it should describe the kind of college you wish to attend.

2. Next, list all the schools you are considering across the top of the page (it's not unusual for students to use two or even three pages).

3. Using any scale you want (e.g., 1 through 10), rate each school according to your criteria. A rough rating is fine at this point. You may need to go back to your brochures, notes, and other resources to refresh your memory about specific items. You may want to weight your ratings, by multiplying the factors more important to you by two or three.

4. Total up your rankings, and when you are done you will probably see a natural break between the schools you'd want to attend and those in which you have a marginal interest.

5. Eliminate the schools at the bottom of your wish list, then go back and fine-tune your ratings.

You should now have a sensible list of schools that you can investigate more thoroughly.

> *tip* **Summertime Work.** The summer before your senior year of high school is the time when you should begin pulling together your short list of schools.

VISITING COLLEGES

After sorting through tons of material and listening to a torrent of well-meaning advice, it's time to get a real view of the schools by making some school visits. This is the single best way to confirm or discard your first impressions and learn more about each school.

Admission people recommend two rounds of visits. In the first round, you want to visit *types* of schools to test out your thoughts on size, location, public versus private, and so on. So plan to visit one or two schools in each category you still question. This doesn't have to involve extensive travel if you have colleges and universities in your region.

At this point you are looking for insight about what types of schools fit you best academically and socially. So, if you are not settled on the size issue, for instance, visit a small liberal arts school (e.g., Williams, Bates, Pomona, Occidental, Swarthmore, or Carlton); to get a taste of a large private research university, visit a school or two like NYU, Syracuse, or USC. Include a visit to your state's main state university campus (Michigan, Texas, Penn State, etc.) to test what a large public university feels like. If you see Ivy in your future, you may have to travel some, but visit a couple of Ivy League campuses. It's reasonable to visit two or even three colleges in a day at this point.

> *tip* **Testing the Waters.** The purpose of first-round visits is just to get a sense of college campuses, not to narrow down your wish list.

The second round of visits should be to the schools you are considering most seriously. Here the purpose is an in-depth look at each one. Plan no more than two visits each day; if possible, spend a day and night at each school.

When to Visit

Visiting schools in the summer has some limitations. True, you can see the campus and the setting, and you can learn a great deal about the academic offerings, but you won't see the school in session with "real" students and faculty.

tip **Timing Is Everything.** Your first-round visits can be accomplished more easily during the summer. For the second round, return to your top three or four choices in the fall of your senior year.

Things to Do before You Visit

1. Read the college viewbook or catalog. Get an idea of how the campus sees itself; you can compare that with what you experience.

2. Prepare a few questions about the campus or academic programs. You may be meeting an admission officer or faculty member.

3. Call to schedule a visit, tour, and interview (if available). Many schools do not offer interviews but hold "group information sessions" instead.

4. Get directions. You don't want to be late.

5. Contact any friends you may know at the school. See if they will be available to show you around.

THINGS TO DO DURING YOUR VISIT

1. Have an interview. If offered, an interview will allow you to learn more about the school and the interviewer to learn something about you.

2. Sit in on an information session. Ask some questions, and listen to what others are asking. Talk with other visiting students about their impressions.

3. Take a campus tour. See what the campus wants you to see.

4. Walk around the campus on your own. Check out classrooms, the library, sports facilities, the student union, and dorms—any places the tour did not cover.

5. Sit in on a class. Get the instructor's permission first, then sit in on a class you think might interest you. It's a great way to learn about the relative formality and tenor of the academic experience.

6. Have a meal. If open, try a cafeteria. It's not Mom's or Dad's home cooking, but will it do? Are there enough options?

7. Read the campus newspaper. This is a great way to get a feel for campus politics, activities, interests, and values.

8. Talk with many students. Most will be ready to tell you what they like about the school and what they think needs improvement.

9. Look for campus safety features. Is there adequate lighting? How far are the dorms from the library? Do you see emergency phones? Are there well-lit transportation/escort stops?

10. Walk around the neighborhood. Check out the local hangouts, bookstores, coffeeshops, and services. Ask about public transportation.

IF YOU CAN'T VISIT

1. Meet with an alum in your area. Most schools will supply you with the names of alumni who live close by.

2. Get a video of the campus. Most schools have one, and it's a way to "see" the campus. If a video is not available through your guidance office, call the campus and ask for one to be sent to you.

3. Attend a college fair. Check to see if the campuses you are interested in will be attending a fair in your area.

4. Go to a regional reception. Many schools hold receptions throughout the country. The format is similar to a campus information session, with admission, financial aid, and student-life representatives.

FINALIZING YOUR LIST

Here's the basic strategy for putting schools on your final list. After all your investigation, the schools on this list should meet your most important criteria. The final list also has to consider relative selectivity:

- Choose one or two "reaches," schools you would love to attend that may be more selective for your record. You never know.

- Choose a few schools that seem within your reach—where you feel you are within the range of selectivity.

- Apply to at least one "safety" school, where you are virtually certain of acceptance.

Be sure to check the accuracy of these designations with your counselor and parents. If you are brave enough to ask, the admission officers at these schools will also help you gauge your chances of acceptance.

> *tip* **How Many Is Enough?** A well-researched process should lead you to apply to five to eight schools. If you can't get your list down to that range, continue to refine your basic criteria. Remember, each application will take money, time, and serious attention.

SUMMARY

In this lesson you learned how to narrow your college choices and how to make the best use of college visits.

APPLY YOURSELF

In this lesson you will learn about completing your admission application, and you will find out your admission options.

COMPLETING YOUR ADMISSION APPLICATION

It's time. This is when students often fall short by not devoting enough time, creativity, or hard work to the application process itself. It may have something to do with misplaced modesty. Listen: you have arrived at this stage in your life, ready to make the transition to the next, after many years of hard work and accomplishment. Most of us have difficulty speaking about ourselves; it seems too boastful or pretentious. Get over it! This is one situation—a job interview is another— where it is important to let the decision makers know how exceptional you are.

Start with the application: if any school on your final list has not sent you an application (usually by September), call or write for one. State schools often send stacks of application materials to high schools within the state. More colleges are using computer disk applications and even the Internet to allow students to apply using the latest technologies.

Pay attention to the various types of application options and deadlines. Make another chart to track these.

ADMISSION OPTIONS

There are five admission options that you need to know about:

1. early action or evaluation

2. early decision

3. regular admission

4. rolling admission

5. open admission

Early action or evaluation allows a student an early answer, but does not require a commitment until May 1.

Early decision is for students who are absolutely certain of their first choice. The deadline for applying is usually earlier than other plans, and the school promises an early reply. Usually, this plan requires students to sign a "statement of commitment" to withdraw all other applications if admission is offered early.

Regular admission is the traditional option for students. You apply by a particular date and expect to learn of the college's decision by a particular date.

Rolling admission is offered by schools that review applications as they arrive and offer admission throughout the cycle, sometimes within several weeks of receipt.

Open admission is offered by schools that are able to admit all students who meet stated minimum requirements—usually two-year community colleges.

Put energy and imagination into the application. After answering the required questions and reporting your grades and test scores, remember that the essay and letters of recommendation will give the reviewer a fuller picture of who you are, what you care about, and what kind of student you will be.

For more information about completing college applications, read Dr. O'Neal Turner's *10 Minute Guide to Getting into College*.

SUMMARY

In this lesson you learned about the admission application and your admission options.

APPLYING FOR FINANCIAL AID

In this lesson you will learn some of the basics about applying for financial aid and institutional scholarships.

REVIEWING COSTS

The cost for tuition and fees for a college education currently ranges between about $5,600 and $19,000 per year, depending on the type of institution, and is increasing about 5 or 6 percent per year. Generally, four-year public institutions are less expensive than their private counterparts, because their tuition is subsidized by state taxes. In addition, there are other expenses to deal with, like room and board, books and supplies, and other incidentals. Any way you cut it, college costs are substantial, and most families must find ways to help finance an education.

By now, you should know the total costs of the colleges on your final list.

> ! **Influence through Money.** A special message to parents: Avoid using your ability or inability to pay for a college as a tool to direct your child to the school that is *your* choice. Many parents say, "I'll only help pay for your education if you go to this one specific college," and that mandate often has poor results.

HOW DOES FINANCIAL AID WORK?

Sometimes it's easier to explain the national debt than the financial aid process, but here's a quick summary:

1. The majority of financial aid is awarded to families on the basis of what is called "demonstrated financial need," a calculation that takes the full cost of attending a college (including tuition, fees, room and board, books, and incidental costs) and subtracts from that what your family can afford to contribute.

2. What you can afford to contribute is based on a standard formula called the "federal methodology" of need analysis. It takes into account your family's income, assets, and liabilities to compute your expected contribution. (Some schools use an alternate formula when it comes to awarding their own funds.)

3. In the end, the amount of financial aid eligibility is determined by subtracting your expected family contribution (EFC) from the total cost of attendance. That amount—your demonstrated financial need—is what colleges seek to provide in the form of a financial aid package.

GET THE RIGHT FORMS, GET THE FORMS RIGHT

Get ready. To qualify for financial aid, you and your family will have to provide one or both of the following:

1. The Free Application for Federal Student Aid (FAFSA). As the name implies, there is no cost for filing. It is the primary financial aid document.

2. Some colleges and universities will also require the Financial Aid PROFILE, which asks for more information and requires a small fee.

Both of these forms are generally available in your college guidance office in the fall. If your college requires the Financial Aid PROFILE, it must be completed in the fall. But you must wait until after January 1 to complete the FAFSA.

In addition, you may need other materials:

- Some colleges also require their own forms. These are usually mailed to you along with the application for admission.

- Your income tax returns and those of your parents may be required. File early and keep photocopies.

- If one or both of your parents own a business or farm, you may be required to submit a Business or Farm Supplement and corporate income tax returns.

- If your parents are separated or divorced, you may be asked to submit a Divorced/Separated Parent's Statement. Schools vary in their policies regarding noncustodial parents' responsibilities for financial support. Check with the financial aid office at each of your target schools.

WHAT'S NEXT?

Within a month or so of returning your FAFSA for processing, you will be sent an official statement called the Student Aid Report (SAR), which details your "expected family contribution." (A similar acknowledgment and report will result from sending in your PROFILE.)

The same information will be forwarded to the schools you have designated. There, the financial aid office will use this information to determine your financial aid package. You should expect either an estimate of financial aid or a final financial aid award by early April from each of your target schools.

tip

Parallel Applications. One of the confusing aspects of the admission process is that it runs parallel with financial aid and scholarship application deadlines. Most schools admit students without regard to family finances. In order to do this legitimately, the processes are kept separate until an admission decision is made.

Since the admission and financial aid application processes are separate, you have to track two sets of important deadlines for each school on your list.

BACK TO THE CHART

A good way to track deadlines is to use another chart. Make a grid with the schools listed down one side and the important deadlines for admission, financial aid, and scholarship applications across the top. Include dates for federal and state forms as well as institutional deadlines.

IMPORTANT POINTS ABOUT FINANCIAL AID

- Do not wait until you have been admitted to apply for financial aid! This is an all-too-common mistake. The lore is that if you don't apply for aid, your chances of being admitted will increase. Not only is this untrue, you may find yourself without any aid.

- Keep up with all deadlines. These vary from school to school, and you do not want to be left out because you "forgot" to send in a crucial form or application. Your chart of deadlines will help.

- Keep a file for each application. It's a good idea to maintain a log of all phone conversations regarding aid. Keep copies of any correspondence you have sent and any sent to you.

- File federal income tax forms in January for both you and your parents. The federal financial aid forms will ask for figures from your 1040 forms. If you have accurate numbers, it will save time later. Otherwise, use your best estimates rather than delay completion of the forms. You can update the forms later.

- Talk with the financial aid office. If you are confused or have special family circumstances you think warrant review, make early contact and keep records of your conversations.

COMPARING COSTS AND FINANCIAL AID OFFERS

You should have about a month before the May 1 "Candidates Reply Deadline" to compare the amount and quality of aid each school will provide you. This is crucial to your choosing the right college. Here's where you'll want to be certain you are comparing apples to apples. It isn't always easy. You'll want to know:

- What is the discount price? The full cost of education includes tuition, fees (which are sometimes considerable), room and board, books, and the official cost of incidentals. The "discount price" is what you will actually pay after grants and scholarships are applied. (Loans don't reduce the amount you pay, just when you pay it.) Keep your eye on this bottom line. The figure may surprise you, as supposedly less-expensive schools may end up costing you more than a school with a higher price tag.

- How will "outside" scholarships be applied? If you are awarded a scholarship from a source other than the college or the government, find out if this amount will be deducted from any loan or grant money in your package. Schools handle this in different ways, and it can greatly affect your final cost.

- Is the package "front-loaded"? Ask if the package offered for the first year can be expected in future years, assuming your income and other factors remain fairly constant. Keep in mind that many schools expect student contributions to increase modestly over four years and will increase the amount of loans awarded each year. And, of course, tuition will likely increase. You'll want to know if aid will keep pace with rising costs.

- Are there any big differences between packages? If there are significant differences in the amount and types of aid you are being offered (particularly any federal aid) from comparably priced schools, ask the financial aid offices to explain them to you.

Some colleges willingly change their offers if they are very interested in you; at other colleges, the offer is firm except for extenuating circumstances.

- Is it enough? Sometimes the financial aid offer does not take into account special expenses you may have or it does not consider a change in your family's financial situation. You should have a frank conversation with the financial aid administrator if you honestly feel you would be unable to attend unless the offer was increased.

- What about payment plans? Many colleges have a range of options for paying tuition and other costs. If this is a concern for you, be certain to inquire, as this may be another way to keep costs from being the sole deciding factor among the colleges you are considering. With the right payment plan, even the most expensive school on your list may become affordable.

! **Dollars and Decisions.** As often as we say that costs should not be a barrier to attending the college of your choice, reality often intervenes. Talk with your family about your situation to see which financial aid offers you have received will work for your family.

SUMMARY

In this lesson you learned about applying for financial aid and some of the ways to compare your financial aid offers.

WHAT TO DO WHEN YOU'RE ACCEPTED

In this lesson you will learn what to do if you've been accepted to some of the colleges you have applied to.

AND, THE ENVELOPE PLEASE . . .

There isn't much in the life of a 17- or 18-year-old that gives you preparation for the day colleges notify you of their decision. You know instinctively as you open up each envelope what they will say: the thin letters are usually nicely worded rejections, while the thick ones are full of forms to return as a newly admitted student.

YOU'RE IN!

What's next? This is where the tables turn. For all these months you've been the one kept in suspense by the colleges, awaiting their answers. Now, it's your turn to evaluate your choices carefully before you notify the colleges of your final selection.

Admission, financial aid, and housing offers should each be assessed with the same care the colleges used in choosing you.

YOUR RIGHTS

The "Statement of Principles of Good Practice" is an ethics agreement among the members of the National Association of College Admissions Counselors. It specifically prohibits member schools from requiring students to pay housing deposits before May 1. (Schools may ask for an earlier deposit, but they will also have to offer you an extension to May 1.) The reason for this prohibition is to protect you from being pressured into making an admission decision before you are ready (and before you've heard from all the colleges you've applied to).

> **!** **Mayday!** You have until May 1, the National Candidate's Reply Date, to do your research and choose one school. At that time, you will usually have to send in a deposit with your acceptance (from a few dollars to a few hundred dollars).

To help you make your final decision, many colleges will offer you an opportunity to come visit again and have one final, close look at the campus before you make your final decision.

If you can make these visits, do so. They're an excellent way to get a second look at the colleges that have accepted you—only this time, without the anxiety of not knowing whether you'll be accepted. This time *you're* in the driver's seat.

If you decide to visit, here are a few things you should do while on campus:

- Visit the financial aid office to complete your file, if something is still needed.

- Speak with a financial aid counselor to talk about your financial aid offer (and, perhaps, to negotiate).

- Visit the housing office and, if known, the dorm where you will be assigned to see what it's like and what you may need to bring.

- Visit the student center or activities office to see what activities you'll get involved in.

- Visit the department office of your major. Depending upon when you visit, you may be able to find out what teachers are teaching what courses in the fall.

- Meet the chair of your department and the department secretary. Both of these people will play a significant role in your student life.

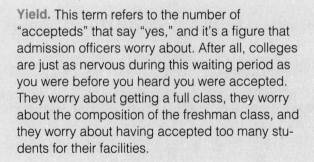

Yield. This term refers to the number of "accepteds" that say "yes," and it's a figure that admission officers worry about. After all, colleges are just as nervous during this waiting period as you were before you heard you were accepted. They worry about getting a full class, they worry about the composition of the freshman class, and they worry about having accepted too many students for their facilities.

STEPS TO TAKE AFTER YOU'VE BEEN ADMITTED

- Evaluate the offers of admission: Have you been admitted to the major or program of your choice? If not, do you have a chance of getting in later? Are there any conditions to your acceptance that you must meet before attending?

- Evaluate the offers of financial aid: Is there sufficient aid for you and your family to make this work?

- Evaluate the offers of housing: Are you guaranteed housing? Is it what you want or need? Have you seen the rooms or spent the night?

- Attend campus open-house programs. Nearly every college will offer you the chance to visit the campus, meet with other admitted students (a great way to see your prospective peers), current students, and faculty. If possible, spend the night; if you cannot stay on campus, then stay nearby. Use these programs to look deep into the college and get a sense of how it might feel to be a student there for four years.

- See your counselor to discuss your offers. Ask for the names of any students from your school who may be attending the colleges you are considering. You may be able to call or see them to get their opinions.

- Sit down with your family. Do a final "reality check" now that the offers are in. Go back through the issues you discussed in your ground-rule conversation.

- Make a decision. Return to your list of criteria (your college "grid"). Some issues are probably more clear to you now, and you may need to adjust your ratings. Evaluate the colleges that have accepted you, using the criteria on the list. But also include your "gut feelings" and the discussions you've had with your family. In the end, you must choose.

SUMMARY

In this chapter you learned what steps to take after you have been accepted into a college.

CONDITIONAL ACCEPTANCES AND REJECTIONS

In this lesson you will learn what conditional acceptances are and some options if you're not accepted.

THE OTHER ANSWERS YOU MIGHT GET

Certainly we hope you get accepted to the college of your choice. But it's possible that instead of getting a straight acceptance, you might receive some other answer. Here are five possibilities:

1. You're in, but not in your major.

2. You're on the wait list.

3. You're not in now, but later . . .

4. You're not in.

5. You're not in *anywhere*.

97

You're In, but Not in Your Major

Some colleges, generally universities with many departments or academic programs, may admit you to the university but not in the major or program you want.

If this is the case, check with the admission office to see under what conditions you will be able to enter the major you want at a later date. The admission office or the academic department itself should be able to give you a good sense of your chances.

 Impacted Majors. Some majors are so popular at some schools that the department cannot accept everybody who's been accepted to the school into that major. This phenomenon is called an "impacted major."

You're on the Wait List

 Wait Lists. The wait list is the college admission equivalent to purgatory: you're not in, you're not out, you're in limbo.

Every college or university has to be concerned about meeting enrollment targets. Admissions is not so much a science as it is an art: making a certain number of offers to applicants, knowing that some percentage will not accept but will go somewhere else. As a result, the college protects its enrollment by placing a number of applicants on a wait list. At some point after May 1, when the college has a better idea of how many students have accepted their offer of admission, the college may decide to take some students off the wait list and admit them.

If you're placed on the wait list at the school you most want to attend:

- Follow the instructions for responding to the wait list offer. Usually you will be asked to return a card. Run to the post office and send it in.

- Secure your place at one of the schools that *did* accept you. *Do not wait until after May 1*. If you are later accepted off the wait list at your first-choice school, you may withdraw from the other college.

- Get more information. Find out if the college rank-orders the wait list. Ask how many students are ordinarily admitted off the wait list and if financial aid is available for them. Find out what the schedule is for notifying students on the wait list and if there are any materials the college would like from you.

- Take the wait list as a challenge. You've come this far in your college selection, and, if you want this school to admit you off the wait list, get busy. Let the college know how well you finished your senior year. If you've previously made contact with someone in the admission office, a faculty member or an alum, this is the time to see if they will work on your behalf by writing a letter to the dean of admission.

> **tip**
>
> **Creative Aggressiveness.** This is one time where you have little to lose by being more aggressive and as creative as possible.

YOU'RE NOT IN NOW, BUT LATER . . .

Many large public universities face enrollment demands they cannot accommodate. Even if you meet or exceed the expected academic and test requirements for admission, you may not be admitted to the term or program to which you applied. Occasionally, you will receive an offer to enroll in a subsequent term.

If it's *the* school and *the* program you most want, accepting this deferred admission may be your best decision. You can use the interim to travel, work, or even begin your studies through extension courses or by attending your local community college.

YOU'RE NOT ADMITTED

First you cry. Then you get mad. Then you recall the line: "I wouldn't belong to any club that would have me as a member." And then you assess the damage. Is it your crushed ego that's causing the pain, or is this the school you really wanted?

tip **Hey, You Never Know . . .** If it's a damaged ego that's hurting, remember that great schools often fail to see the potential talent in their applicant pools. Steven Spielberg, the award-winning movie director, was turned down three times by the cinema school at USC (which recently gave him an honorary degree).

If you are absolutely convinced this is the right college for you and that a grave miscarriage of justice has been done, you may wish to appeal the decision. Each college will have its own policy, so it's best to check the college's literature.

Appeals. Generally, appeals are not encouraged unless some new, compelling information has surfaced since your original application.

YOU'RE NOT IN *Anywhere*

If this is your situation, it will say more about your search process than it will about you as a person. It means your choices were not realistic.

The question now is, what are your options? Here are three that you can try at one of the colleges:

- You can appeal.

- You can ask to be admitted on a probationary basis.

- You can ask to be reconsidered after doing some additional academic work during the summer or fall.

Most likely, you should look at some other options. Here are four more:

- You can try to get accepted by another four-year college. NACAC conducts the *Space Availability Survey* each May to see what colleges and universities are still accepting students after May 1. Look on the list to see if you can find a good match. (If your counselor doesn't have a copy of the survey, you can write NACAC at 1631 Prince Street, Alexandria, VA 22314-2818.)

- Consider completing a post–high school graduate year at a college preparatory school to improve your chances of admission the following year. Be sure to speak with your counselor and an admission officer at your target college to make a realistic plan.

- Attend a community college and plan a transfer curriculum with the help of a counselor. Most community colleges accept students for enrollment up to the very last minute.

- Work for a year. Seek employment that will make you a more attractive candidate for admission to your target college.

Summary

In this lesson you learned what conditional acceptances are, and some of your options if you're not accepted at the school of your choice.

LESSON

15

WRAPPING IT
ALL UP

*In this lesson you will learn what the colleges that have
accepted you are expecting you to do before you enroll.*

RSVP

It may seem obvious, but all the colleges that have accepted
you expect you to respond with your answer by May 1.

You probably won't need much of a reminder to notify the
college you will be attending of your answer. But the colleges
you are turning down (sounds good, doesn't it?) also deserve
an answer.

 **Reply Card.** Usually, the letter of admission will
include a response card to send back to the ad-
missions office. Send in your responses by May
1, even to the schools you are turning down (doing so may allow another candidate to get admitted).

STAYING ON TOP OF IT

Once you've been accepted and have sent in your deposit, you will start receiving information from other parts of campus. Housing, financial aid, orientation, parking, health services, and other offices are likely to send you materials and ask for responses. Don't delay.

tip   **Final Transcripts.** Be certain that your high school sends your final high school transcript, Advanced Placement test results, and documentation of summer course work.

The gap between college-level study and what is expected of you in high school—even at the best prep schools—is already fairly significant. If you catch "senioritis" and blow off your classes for the rest of your senior year, three possible things can happen. None is pleasant for you.

- You may jeopardize your admission, because the college that admitted you will expect you to maintain the high standard they saw during the admission process.

- You may not graduate from high school, thus defeating your entire college search.

- You may find yourself getting off to a shaky start in the fall, out of practice and out of sync.

SUMMER PLANNING

Every college will provide some help to you in making the transition to college. Orientation programs are offered through the summer or before the start of classes. You can make the most of these if you do some thinking ahead about majors, courses, internships, and activities.

> ***tip*** **Away for the Summer?** If you are going to be gone during the summer preceding your enrollment, make arrangements for your parents or someone else to handle the many requests you'll be getting. Some will require an immediate response.

THINGS TO DO IN THE SUMMER BEFORE YOUR FRESHMAN YEAR

- Take your parents out to dinner. Thank them for their help and for putting up with you through this process.

- Write a note to everyone who helped you in your quest for the right college. Let each know your plans and thank them for their part in your success.

- Think about what kind of roommate you want; you may get to choose.

- Set up a communication plan with your family. Arrange for an E-mail account, an 800 number for home, or a set time and day to call.

- Arrange an allowance, use of a credit card for larger purchases, and a way to get cash for small purchases.

- Help someone else who is just starting the college search. You're an expert now.

SUMMARY

In this chapter you learned what to do once you have decided to enroll in a particular college.

COLLEGE SEARCH CALENDAR

The college search process will tax all your organizational skills. Choosing the right college involves self-awareness, family dynamics, making good use of your resources, research, evaluation, and reams of paper. This calendar will help you organize it all.

10TH GRADE

This is the year you begin the college search process, by preparation and some exploration.

- See your guidance counselor about starting your college search. Ask about any college fairs or programs in your area to get a head start on looking at possibilities.

- Ask about dates and then sign up to take the Preliminary Scholastic Achievement Test/National Merit Scholarship Qualifying Test (PSAT/NMSQT) offered for sophomores in October.

- If you are completing any courses that will prepare you for the SAT II tests, sign up in March for the May tests, or April for the June tests. Your counselor will have a schedule and the registration forms.

- In May or June, take the SAT II test, if appropriate.

- Prepare for your fall class registration by talking with your counselor about the most appropriately challenging courses.

- Consider registering for a community college course to enhance your record and give you a taste of college.

11th Grade

This is it. Use this year to deepen both your record and your search for the right college.

September

- Set up a time for your "ground-rule conversation" with your family.

- If you haven't done so yet, get to know your counselor and the college guidance resources available at your high school and in your community.

- Find out when and where the PSAT/NMSQT is being given. Mark the dates and the deadline for registration.

- Find out from your counselor when college fairs and college visits to your high school will take place. Plan to be there.

OCTOBER

- Begin your broad list of possible college options.

- Schedule some "round one" visits to nearby universities and colleges to explore different types of schools.

DECEMBER

- Talk with college friends home for the holidays. Ask if you can visit them later in the year to see what their colleges are like.

- Use the holiday vacation to start searching through the materials recommended in this book.

JANUARY

- Plan any SAT I and II or ACT tests for this year by marking them (and the registration deadlines) on your calendar.

FEBRUARY

- If you are going to take the SAT I in March, remember the February deadline.

- If you haven't done so already, buy or borrow some general guidebooks to colleges and universities.

MARCH

- Plan spring-vacation visits to colleges on your list.
- Start organizing your college files for each school.
- Start your "grid" of college criteria and begin matching it to schools you are exploring.
- Register for the May SAT I or II, if appropriate.

APRIL

- Evaluate, sort, and organize the avalanche of material sent to you by colleges and universities.
- Respond to the colleges that interest you most, usually by sending back a card.
- Begin planning your senior-year classes, including any Advanced Placement courses, a fourth year of math, and a lab science.
- Register for the June SAT I or II, if appropriate.

MAY

- SAT I and II are given in early May.
- Register for the June test date for the Test of English as a Foreign Language (TOEFL), if needed.
- Plan your summer college search activities: some college visits and further study and inquiries.
- Keep talking to your parents about college plans.

SUMMER

- Write or call any target colleges that did not contact you and ask for additional information. Don't assume they are not interested in you; some schools mail only to a small group of students.

- Visit colleges. Plan this with your parents to keep communication open.

- Complete any audition tapes, art portfolios, or special materials you anticipate will be required for admission to special programs or majors.

- Approach any "out-of-school" people you hope to have write a letter of recommendation for you. Give them some warning that you may need a letter in the fall.

- Begin thinking about, or even writing, a personal statement that many colleges will want as part of the college admission application.

12TH GRADE

Get ready: This is the hardest year of the college admission process. Not only are there countless details to be tracked for college applications, it is also a busy year for social and academic activities.

SEPTEMBER

- Mark your calendar for any SAT I and II or ACT test and registration dates.

- Ask your guidance counselor about this year's schedule for college representatives' visits and any regional college fairs. Mark these on your calendar as well.

- Request applications from the schools on your target list.

- Plan your fall college visits. Find out about any special programs, open houses, or overnight programs at your target schools.

OCTOBER

- Register for the December SAT I or II, if necessary.

- Put your "grid" of important dates together for the admission, financial aid, scholarship, and housing deadlines of each target school.

- Ask for teacher and counselor recommendations now. Give them sufficient time to do a good job for you.

- If you haven't yet started, begin planning your college essay(s).

- Pick up the Financial Aid PROFILE Registration form. Complete it if any of the colleges you will be applying to require it.

NOVEMBER

- SAT I and II are given in early November.
- Registration for the December ACT is this month.
- Plan for any early application deadlines.

DECEMBER

- SAT I and II and the ACT are given in December.
- Check with your counselor and teachers about recommendations.
- Be certain that your transcripts are being sent to your final list of colleges.
- Complete any applications that are due in January or February.
- Pick up the FAFSA financial aid application from your counselor.
- Attend any workshops on applying for financial aid. Take your parents.
- Use the holidays to concentrate on talking with friends who attend your final list of colleges.

JANUARY

- Complete any remaining applications. Keep copies.

- File income taxes and encourage your parents to do the same, if at all possible. Keep copies.
- Complete any financial aid applications you need to and send them in. Keep copies.

FEBRUARY

- Make certain that your applications have been received. Most schools will mail an acknowledgment. If you don't receive one, call the school.

APRIL

- Compare all the offers of admission, financial aid, and housing that will arrive this month. Put them all on the "grid."
- Plan your last set of visits, concentrating on your first-choice schools. Plan on at least a full day, and stay overnight if possible.
- Follow up on any questions regarding financial aid or housing.
- Make your decision and send the required notice and deposit to your first-choice college.
- Send back any "wait list" cards you receive.
- Notify the other colleges that have offered you admission of your plans. This may help another applicant come off the wait list.

MAY

- Take any appropriate Advanced Placement exams.

- Stay on top of any remaining business from your new school (housing, financial aid, orientation, advising, etc.).

- Be sure to let everyone who has helped you through this process know of your plans and thank them for their help.

JUNE

- Be certain that your final high school transcript has been sent to your new school.

- Get a summer job. Help your parents pay for the next four years of your life.

- Have a great (and safe) high school graduation.

- Get ready for college.

APPENDIX B

COLLEGE CHECKLIST

Use this grid to help you evaluate how well your college choices fit your criteria.

Criteria	College A Name:	College B Name:	College C Name:	College D Name:
Faculty				
Academic programs				
Class size				
Size of college				
Class availability				
Library				
Guidance				
Location				
Student body				
Security				
Housing				
Food				
Health care				
Values				
Other criteria:				
TOTAL				

Appendix C

Common College Majors

Here is a selected list of common courses of study at many colleges and universities:

Accounting

Advertising

Aerospace Sciences

African Studies

Agricultural Economics

Agricultural Engineering

Agronomy/Soil and Crop Sciences

American Studies

Animal Sciences

Anthropology

Arabic

Archeology

Architecture

Art/Fine Arts

Art History

Art Therapy

Asian/Oriental Studies

Astronomy

Atmospheric Sciences

Aviation Technology

Behavioral Sciences

Biochemistry

Bioengineering

Biology/Biological Sciences

Biotechnology

Botany/Plant Sciences

Broadcasting

Business Administration

Business Economics

Carpentry

Ceramic Art and Design

Chemical Engineering

Chemistry

Child Care/Child and Family Studies

Child Psychology/Child Development

Chinese

City/Community/Regional Planning

Civil Engineering

Classics

Communication

Comparative Literature

Computer Engineering

Computer Graphics

Computer Science

Conservation

Court Reporting

Creative Writing

Criminal Justice

Culinary Arts

Dairy Sciences

Dance

Dental Services

Dietetics

Drafting and Design

Early Childhood Education

East Asian Studies

East European Studies

Ecology

Economics

Education

Electrical Engineering

Elementary Education

Engineering

English

Entomology

Environmental Sciences

Ethnic Studies

European Studies

Family and Consumer Sciences

Fashion Design and Technology

Film Studies

Finance/Banking

Fire Science

Fish and Game Management

Food Sciences

Forensic Sciences

Forestry

French

Genetics

Geography

Geology

German

Gerontology

Graphic Arts

Greek

Health Education

Hebrew

Hispanic Studies

History

Home Economics

Horticulture

Hotel and Restaurant Management

Human Development

Humanities

Industrial Administration

Information Science

Interior Design

International Business

International Relations

Islamic Studies

Italian

Japanese

Journalism

Judaic Studies

Landscape Architecture/Design

Latin American Studies

Law Enforcement/Police Sciences

Pre-Law Sequence

Liberal Arts

Library Science

Linguistics

Literature

Marine Biology

Marketing/Retailing/Merchandising

Mathematics

Mechanical Engineering

Pre-Medicine Sequence

Medieval Studies

Metallurgy

Meteorology

Microbiology

Military Science

Modern Languages

Molecular Biology

Music

Native American Studies

Natural Sciences

Near and Middle Eastern Studies

Nuclear Engineering

Nursing

Nutrition

Oceanography

Optometry

Ornamental Horticulture

Painting/Drawing

Parks Management

Peace Studies

Pharmacology

Philosophy

Physical Education

Physical Therapy

Physics

Physiology

Political Science/Government

Psychology

Public Affairs and Policy Studies

Public Health

Real Estate

Religious Education

Retail Management

Romance Languages

Russian and Slavic Studies

Sculpture

Social Science

Social Work

Sociology

Soil Conservation

Spanish

Speech Therapy

Sports Administration

Sports Medicine

Statistics

Textiles and Clothing

Theater Arts/Drama

Theology

Tourism and Travel

Urban Studies

Pre-Veterinary Medicine Sequence

Veterinary Sciences

Wildlife Management

Women's Studies

INDEX

A

academic considerations
  class availability, 48
  class size, 46–48
  faculty, 42–43
  guidance services, 50
  learning environment, 41–42
  libraries, 49
  majors, 44–45, 121–123
accepting admission, 105
admission officers, 22
admission options, 78–79
admission policies, 67
Advanced Placement exams, 117
alumni, 22, 32
American Council on Education, 2
applications, 77–78
  accepting admission, 105
  admission options, 78–79
  conditional acceptances
    alternative majors, 98
    postponing admission, 100
    waiting lists, 98–100
  financial aid, 83–85
  National Candidate's Reply Date, 92
  rejection letters, 100–101
  response letters, 91–93
availability of classes, 48

B

black colleges, 37

C

calendar for college planning, 109–117
campus safety, 58–59
Campus Security Act of 1990, 58
campus visits, 7–9, 23, 55, 70–71, 93

125

G

grants, 68
guidance counselors, 20
guidance services on campus,
50

H

health services, 62–63
high school preparation, 17
  guidance counselors, 20
  transcripts, 106

I

independent counselors, 21
Internet, 29–30, 49
  libraries, 49

K

*K and W Guide to Colleges for
the Learning Disabled,* 28

L

learning environment, 41–42
letters of acceptance, 91–93
  accepting admission, 105
  conditional acceptances
    alternative majors, 98
    *postponing admission,
    100*
    waiting lists, 98–100
  rejection letters, 100–101

libraries, 49
living arrangements, 59–62
  meals, 61–62
loans, 68
location, 54–57

M

magazines, 30–31
majors, 44–45
  common majors, 121–123
  conditional acceptances, 98
meals, 61–62
men's colleges, 36
merit-based financial aid, 67
military schools, 38
mission statements, 63
Money, 30

N

NACAC (National Association
  of College Admissions
  Counselors), 21, 32, 92
narrowing college choices, 75
National Candidate's Reply
  Date, 92
need-based financial aid, 67
nonacademic considerations
  campus safety, 58–59
  health services, 62–63
  location, 54–57
  meals, 61–62
  residential concerns, 59–61
  student body, 57–58
  value systems, 63–64